Sharks

Patricia Kendell

HODDER
Wayland

An imprint of Hodder Children's Books

Alligators Chimpanzees Dolphins Elephants
Gorillas Grizzly Bears Leopards Lions
Pandas Polar Bears Sharks Tigers

© 2002 White-Thomson Publishing Ltd

Produced for Hodder Wayland by White-Thomson Publishing Ltd

Editor: Kay Barnham
Designer: Tim Mayer
Consultants: Dr Sian Pullen – Head of WWF's Marine & Coastal
   Policy Team; Callum Rankine – International Species Officer
   at WWF-UK.
Language Consultant: Norah Granger – Senior Lecturer in Primary
   Education at the University of Brighton
Picture research: Shelley Noronha – Glass Onion Pictures

Published in Great Britain in 2002 by Hodder Wayland,
an imprint of Hodder Children's Books.

Photograph acknowledgements:
Ardea London Ltd 18 (Don Hadden), 12 & 20 (Ralf Kiefner),
13 & 24 (Ken Lucas), 7 (Pat Morris), 14 (Douglas David Seifert),
29 (Mark Spencer), 6, 16, 23, 25 & 26 (Ron & Valerie Taylor),
19 & 32 (Valerie Taylor); BBC 5 (Michael Pitts),
4 (Bruce Rasner/Rotman); FLPA 1 & 17 (Mammal Fund
Earthviews), 8 (D P Wilson); NHPA 21 (Mark Bowler);
Oxford Scientific Films 9; Still Pictures 11 (Yves Lefevre),
10, 15, 22, 28 (Jeffrey Rotman).

British Library Cataloguing in Publication Data
Kendell, Patricia
   1. Sharks - Juvenile literature
   I. Title II. Kay Barnham
   597.3

ISBN: 0 7502 4135 7

Printed and bound in Hong Kong

Hodder Children's Books
A division of Hodder Headline Limited
338 Euston Road, London NW1 3BH

Produced in association with WWF-UK.
WWF-UK registered charity number 1081247.
A company limited by guarantee number 4016725.
Panda device © 1986 WWF ® WWF registered trademark owner.

Contents

Where sharks live

Sharks live in the seas around the world. Some, like this strange megamouth shark, spend much of their time in the **depths** of the sea.

The basking shark can live in deep water, but comes to shallow water near the coast in summer.

The shark family

Sharks belong to the fish family. There are about 400 different types. The whale shark is the biggest fish in the sea.

Others, like this dogfish shark, are only one metre long.

Baby sharks

Some sharks hatch from eggs laid in egg purses,
like these dogfish. Most sharks hatch from eggs
inside their mother. Then they are born like humans.

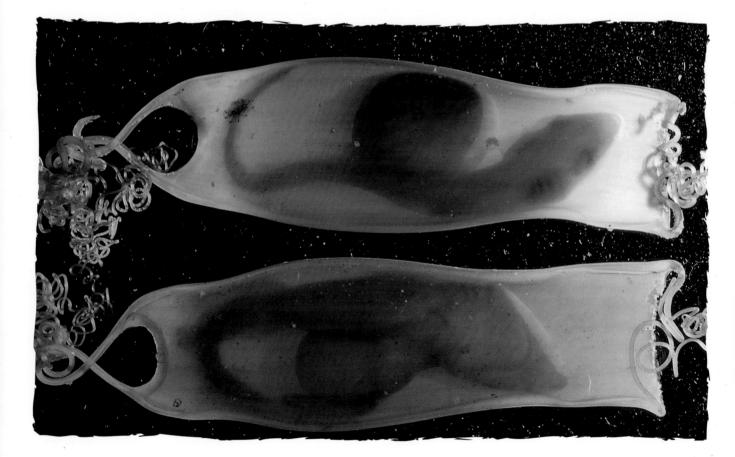

When they are born, baby sharks look like
miniature adult sharks. Their mother does not
care for them – they must look after themselves.

Finding the way

Sharks can see, hear, smell, taste and touch.
This hammerhead shark has a very good view
of the sea all around!

Sharks can easily **detect** movements made in the water,
even if the **prey** is a long way off.

On the move

The great white shark
pushes through the water,
flicking its great forked
tail from side to side.

The leopard shark is very **flexible**.
It can turn around in small places.

Teeth and food

The sand tiger shark has long curved teeth,
which it uses to **snare** fish and **squid**.

The basking shark swims slowly, using its mouth to catch lots of small plants and animals.

Out of sight

Angel sharks hide in the sand on the seabed
waiting to snap up a passing fish.

The great white shark's dark back and light underside help to **disguise** it in the water.

Hunter sharks

Sharks like the great white are powerful hunters.
They can eat a whole seal in one meal.

When great whites find a prey, they speed up
and close in.

In for the kill!

The great white shark's huge jaws open wide,
showing their many saw-like teeth.

This shark is being fed bait, so scientists can see how it eats.
As they snap up prey, great whites roll their eyes back into
their head to stop them being scratched.

Shark attack!

Sharks do sometimes attack and kill people, but this is very rare.

If great whites do attack it is usually because they mistake people on surf boards for seals or turtles.

Threats...

People are a shark's main enemy.
Hunters compete to see how many
shark jaws they can collect.

Sharks are also killed for their meat, fins, skin and liver oil. Shark teeth are made into jewellery.

...and dangers

Sharks get caught in nets that are set to catch other fish or put up to protect surfers and swimmers.